Famous Myths and Legends of the World

Myths and Legends of

CHINA

WORLD
BOOK

a Scott Fetzer company
Chicago
www.worldbook.com

WORLD BOOK and the GLOBE DEVICE are registered trademarks or trademarks of World Book, Inc.

World Book, Inc.
180 North LaSalle Street
Suite 900
Chicago, Illinois 60601
USA

For information about other World Book publications, visit our website at **www.worldbook.com** or call **1-800-967-5325**.

Library of Congress Cataloging-in-Publication Data

Myths and legends of China.
     pages cm. -- (Famous myths and legends of the world)
   Summary: "Myths and legends from China. Features include information about the history and culture behind the myths, pronunciations, lists of deities, word glossary, further information, and index"-- Provided by publisher.
   Includes index.
   ISBN 978-0-7166-2632-9
   1. Mythology, Chinese--Juvenile literature. 2. China--Folklore--Juvenile literature. I. World Book, Inc. II. Series: Famous myths and legends of the world.
   BL1825.M98 2015
   398.20951--dc23
                                        2015014762

Set ISBN: 978-0-7166-2625-1
E-book ISBN: 978-0-7166-2644-2 (EPUB3)

Printed in China by PrintWORKS Global Services,
Shenzhen, Guangdong
2nd printing May 2016

Writer: Scott A. Leonard

Staff for World Book, Inc.
Executive Committee
President: Jim O'Rourke
Vice President and Editor in Chief: Paul A. Kobasa
Vice President, Finance: Donald D. Keller
Vice President, Marketing: Jean Lin
Director, International Sales: Kristin Norell
Director, Licensing Sales: Edward Field
Director, Human Resources: Bev Ecker

Editorial
Manager, Annuals/Series Nonfiction: Christine Sullivan
Managing Editor, Annuals/Series Nonfiction:
    Barbara Mayes
Administrative Assistant: Ethel Matthews
Manager, Indexing Services: David Pofelski
Manager, Contracts & Compliance
    (Rights & Permissions): Loranne K. Shields

Manufacturing/Production
Manufacturing Manager: Sandra Johnson
Production/Technology Manager: Anne Fritzinger
Proofreader: Nathalie Strassheim

Graphics and Design
Senior Art Director: Tom Evans
Coordinator, Design Development and Production:
    Brenda Tropinski
Senior Designers: Matthew Carrington,
    Isaiah W. Sheppard, Jr.
Media Researcher: Jeff Heimsath
Manager, Cartographic Services: Wayne K. Pichler
Senior Cartographer: John M. Rejba

Staff for Brown Bear Books Ltd
Managing Editor: Tim Cooke
Editorial Director: Lindsey Lowe
Children's Publisher: Anne O'Daly
Design Manager: Keith Davis
Designer: Mike Davis
Picture Manager: Sophie Mortimer

Picture credits
t=top, c=center, b=bottom, l=left, r=right
4bl, Alamy; 5t, Shutterstock; 6, WORLD BOOK map; 7, Topfoto; 8-9, Shutterstock; 10t, Bridgeman Images; 10b, Dreamstime; 11t, Topfoto; 11b, Alamy; 12-13, Shutterstock; 14, Thinkstock; 16, Corbis; 17t, Alamy; 17b, WORLD BOOK illustration; 18-19, Alamy; 21, Bridgeman Images; 22, Topfoto; 22-23t, Shutterstock; 23bl, Shutterstock; 23br, Corbis; 24-25, Shutterstock; 26-27, Corbis; 28t Shutterstock; 28bl, Bridgeman Images; 29t, Mary Evans Picture Library; 29l, Thinkstock; 30-31, Shutterstock; 32-33, Alamy; 34t, Topfoto; 34b, Thinkstock; 35t, Mary Evans Picture Library; 35b, Corbis; 36-37, Shutterstock; 38-39, Shutterstock; 40t, Alamy; 40b, Shutterstock; 41t, Corbis; 41b, Shutterstock; 42-43, Corbis; 44-46, Corbis; 46-47t, Alamy; 47b, Corbis; 48-51, Corbis; 52t, Art Archive; 52b, LOOK die Bildagentur der Fotografen; 53, Bridgeman Images; 55, Alamy; 56-58, Shutterstock; 59t, Alamy; 59b, Corbis; 61 Alamy; back cover, Shutterstock.

CONTENTS

A threatening sea dragon is kept at bay by the protection of the Tin Hau Temple, in a wall painting in Stanley, a town in Hong Kong.

© Robert Harrison, Alamy Images

Note to Readers:

Phonetic pronunciations have been inserted into the myths and legends in this volume to make reading the stories easier and to give the reader some of the flavor of the ancient Chinese culture the stories represent. See page 64 for a pronunciation key.

The myths and legends retold in this volume are written in a creative way to provide an engaging reading experience and approximate the artistry of the originals. Many of these stories were not written down but were recited by storytellers from generation to generation. Even when some of the stories came to be written down they likely did not feature phonetic pronunciations for challenging names and words! We hope the inclusion of this material will improve rather than distract from your experience of the stories.

Some of the figures mentioned in the myths and legends in this volume are described on page 60 in the section "Deities of China." In addition, some unusual words in the text are defined in the Glossary on page 62.

INTRODUCTION

Since the earliest times, people have told stories to try to explain the world in which they lived. These stories are known as myths. Myths try to answer such questions as, How was the world created? Who were the first people? Where did the animals come from? Why does the sun rise and set? Why is the land devastated by storms or drought? Today, people often rely on science to answer many of these questions. But in earlier times—and in some parts of the world today—people explained natural events using stories about gods, goddesses, spirits of nature, and heroes.

Myths are different from folk tales and legends. Folk tales are fictional stories about people or animals. Most of these tales are not set in any particular time or place, and they begin and end in a certain way. For example, many English folk tales begin with the phrase "Once upon a time" and end with "They lived happily ever after." Legends are set in the real world, in the present or the historical past. They distort the truth but are based on real people or events.

From The World of the Monkey King, page 58

Myths, in contrast, typically tell of events that have taken place in the remote past. Unlike legends, myths have also played—and often continue to play—an important role in a society's religious life. Although legends may have religious themes, most are not religious in nature. The people of a society may tell folk tales and legends for amusement, without believing them. But they usually consider their myths sacred and completely true.

Most myths concern *divinities* or *deities* (divine beings). These divinities have powers far greater than those of any human being. At the same time, however, many gods, goddesses, and heroes of mythology have human characteristics. They are guided by such emotions as love and jealousy, and they may experience birth and death. Mythological figures may even look like human beings. Often, the human qualities of a culture's divinities reflect that society's ideals. Good gods and goddesses have the qualities a society admires, and evil ones have the qualities it dislikes. In myths, the actions of these divinities influence the world of humans for better or for worse.

From The World of the Chinese Zodiac, page 28

Myths can sometimes seem very strange. They sometimes seem to take place in a world that is both like our world and unlike it. Time can go backward and forward, so it is sometimes difficult to tell in what order events happen. People may be dead and alive at the same time.

Myths were originally passed down from generation to generation by word of mouth. Partly for this reason, there are often different versions of the same story. Many myths across cultures share similar themes, such as a battle between good and evil. But the myths of a society generally reflect the landscape, climate, and society in which the storytellers lived. Myths tell people about their distant history. They show people how to behave in the world and find their way. As teaching tools, myths help to prepare children for adulthood.

A people's folklore includes its myths, legends, and traditional folk tales and songs. Folklore also includes customs and beliefs. Children learn about their folklore from teachers and older people in their society. Every society around the world has a folklore that is special to it.

Myths and Legends of China

China was home to some of the world's earliest civilizations. By about 10,000 B.C., a number of cultures had developed in this area. From two of them—the Yangshao and the Longshan—a distinctly Chinese civilization gradually emerged. The Yangshao culture reached the peak of its development about 3000 B.C. The culture, which extended from the central valley of the Huang He to the present-day province of Gansu, was based on millet farming. (Millet is a type of grain.) The *silt* (particles of soil) deposited by the river's floods created fertile plains for farming. About the same time, the Longshan culture spread over much of what is now the eastern third of modern-day China. The Longshan people lived in walled communities, cultivated rice, and raised cattle and sheep.

China's early civilizations emerged along the fertile valleys of the Huang He (Yellow River) in the north of the country and alongside the Yangtze River farther south.

The Shang, the first Chinese culture that left written records, emerged in northern China around 1600 B.C. The populations of northern and southern China first began to mingle under the following Zhou dynasty, which ruled China for around 800 years, from about 1045 to 256 B.C. The country was unified for the first time by Shi Huangdi, a Qin leader, between 230 and 222 B.C. He named himself emperor in 221 B.C. His name means *first emperor*.

Ancient China had many different cultures and many different deities. Some date back to the country's earliest cultures. Others joined the Chinese *pantheon* (collection of deities) after Buddhism arrived in China from India. Taoism, which developed in China probably around 400 B.C., also strongly influenced Chinese mythology.

Although many of the stories in this book appear simple at first glance, they are layered with meaning. Retellings of the stories often reveal new insights. By studying myths, we can learn how different societies have answered basic questions about the world and the individual's place in it. By examining myths, we can better understand the feelings and values that bind members of society into one group. We can also compare the myths of various cultures to discover how these cultures differ and how they resemble one another.

From The World of the Warring States, page 22

P'AN KU
Creates the World

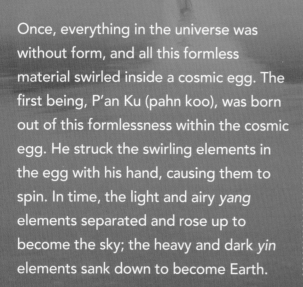

The Chinese story of P'an Ku, the first being, tells how he created Earth and the sky.

Once, everything in the universe was without form, and all this formless material swirled inside a cosmic egg. The first being, P'an Ku (pahn koo), was born out of this formlessness within the cosmic egg. He struck the swirling elements in the egg with his hand, causing them to spin. In time, the light and airy *yang* elements separated and rose up to become the sky; the heavy and dark *yin* elements sank down to become Earth.

P'an Ku changed as the universe changed within the cosmic egg. He changed nine times a day. Sometimes he was a god in the sky; sometimes he was a holy being on Earth.

To keep the sky and Earth from mixing again, P'an Ku grew each day. Each day, he pushed the sky and Earth farther apart. This continued for 18,000 years until there was no more room in the

cosmic egg. Then the egg broke, and the universe blossomed into the shape it still has today.

Satisfied that sky and Earth had now achieved their permanent places, P'an Ku rested, for he was weary in body and spirit. As he slept, his body died and gave further shape to Earth. His eyes became the sun and moon. His arms and legs became the four great mountains that mark the four directions. His blood flowed as rivers. His flesh became soil, and his hair became trees. His breath formed the sky and winds. And the lice that had previously crawled over his body became humans.

Some say the spirit of P'an Ku remains on Earth. When he is content, the weather is fine. But when he is sad or gloomy, storms roll in.

The World of P'AN KU

People lived in what is now China long before the beginning of written history. Early human beings probably inhabited parts of eastern China more than 1 million years ago. By about 10,000 B.C., a number of cultures had developed in this area. From two of them—the Yangshao and the Longshan—a distinctly Chinese civilization gradually emerged.

CIVILIZATION

Some of the oldest evidence of human beings mastering fire, creating music, and developing writing comes from China. Chinese tradition says that civilization began there with the Xia (SHEE ah) dynasty in the 2100's B.C. Archaeologists have found evidence of the Xia, but scholars debate whether modern Chinese descended from this Bronze Age culture. The Shang (shahng) emerged about 1766 B.C. They were the first *dynasty* (series of rulers from one family) of the historical period. By the 300's B.C., there were seven rival states in eastern China. In 221 B.C., the Qin (chihn) state defeated the last of its rival states and established China's first empire controlled by a strong central government.

The Qianlong (chee EHN loong) Emperor, who reigned in the mid-1700's, holds a brush used for *calligraphy* (fine handwriting). The Chinese have traditionally considered calligraphy the highest form of art. It has long been closely linked with poetry and painting. The use of a brush for writing in China became common during the Han dynasty (206 B.C.-A.D. 220). The earliest examples of Chinese writing date from about 1500 to 1045 B.C., during the Shang dynasty. The writing was inscribed on pieces of bone or turtle shell.

A drummer beats time for rowers in a Chinese wood carving showing dragon boat racing. Long, narrow, highly decorated dragon boats date back thousands of years. The ancient Chinese raced the boats to honor the dragon, an object of worship and a symbol of water, to ensure that farmers would receive enough rain for a successful harvest.

Chinese *sages* (wise people) admire a scroll decorated with the yin and yang symbol. Yin and yang are the two main forces of nature in Chinese philosophy, martial arts, and medicine. Yin and yang are *complementary* (cooperative) forces that work together to produce the balance of forces of the visible world. Yin is associated with such qualities as dark, sinking, cool, reactive, and the feminine. Yang is associated with such qualities as bright, rising, warm, active, and the masculine. Everything, including humanity, has both yin and yang elements. Originally, the terms *yin* and *yang* referred to the shady and sunny sides of a mountain slope. Eventually, the names became general terms representing complementary qualities.

QI

One of the basic concepts of Chinese traditional medicine is *qi* (*chee*). Qi is a basic life force that is a combination of energy and matter— the stuff that all things are made of. Everything in the material world is made of qi, which also gives movement to and changes matter. According to ancient Chinese texts, all qi is in a relatively yin or yang state.

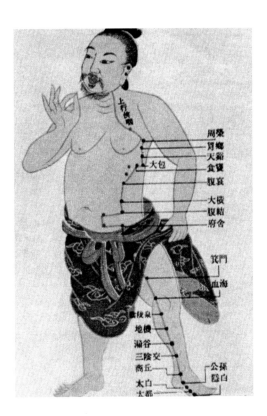

Dots along one side of an illustration trace a meridian in acupuncture, a form of traditional Chinese medicine. Meridians are believed to be channels through which qi— energy—travels through the body. Acupuncturists insert needles at points along meridians to restore the balance between yin and yang in their patients. Acupuncturists believe disease and pain occur as a result of an imbalance between these forces.

HUO YI,
the Divine Archer

Huo Yi became a great mythological hero when he used his arrows to save people from a terrible drought caused by the presence of 10 suns in the sky—though he paid the price for angering the King Father.

Once on a faraway island, 10 boy-suns played in the branches of a mulberry tree. The tree was so vast its branches reached to heaven, and its trunk was so large that 1,000 men, holding hands, could not encircle it. This tree was the home of Di Jun (dee joon), the King Father of the East; his wife, Xi Wangmu (shee wahn moo), the Queen Mother of the West; and their 10 boy-suns. Each day, the Queen Mother would ride to the top of the mulberry tree in a chariot drawn by six dragons. She would pick up one of her boy-suns and then travel all day across the sky from east to west, sending life-giving light to Earth. By the

time their chariot disappeared beyond the western mountains, the young boy-sun would be asleep. His mother would take him back to the mulberry tree and tuck all her children into bed for the night.

After 100 years, this routine grew tiresome for the boy-suns. They wanted to play in the sky together. So one morning, before the Queen Mother of the West could pick up one of the boy-suns for a ride across the sky, all 10 of them flew off, laughing. They had a wonderful time playing together. But while the boy-suns played, the people of Earth suffered. Ten bright suns playing in the sky soon created a blazing light and terrible heat. The rich, moist soil of Earth turned to dust. The tall crops withered. The abundant waters of the rivers and lakes began to boil. The animals of the forests and the animals of the fields were driven mad by their thirst and then died. The bright sky dazzled the eyes of the people, blinding those who did not hide inside. Even in their huts, the people were too frightened and hot to move.

In their suffering, the people turned to Emperor Yao (yow), who prayed night and day to the King Father of the East for relief. The King Father tried to persuade the boys to come home. But the boy-suns were reckless and

disobedient and ignored their father. Exasperated, the King Father sent for Huo Yi (how yee), the Divine Archer, and gave him a scarlet bow and a quiver filled with 10 white arrows.

"Huo Yi," the King Father of the East commanded, "restore order to Earth. Use this bow to frighten my sons into obedience."

But when Huo Yi reached Earth, he was shocked by the devastation. "The time for peaceful measures is past," raged Huo Yi. "These suns must be destroyed or all life on Earth will perish!"

Drawing back his bow, Huo Yi let fly the first of his 10 arrows. It struck one of the boy-suns, who exploded and fell to Earth in a fireball. Huo Yi loosed another arrow. And another. Now there were six boy-suns. Then five. Then four. People began to peek out of their homes to cheer on Huo Yi.

But Emperor Yao worried that Huo Yi, in his anger, would destroy all the boy-suns and plunge Earth into everlasting darkness. So the emperor sent a soldier to secretly remove one of Huo Yi's arrows from his quiver.

When there was only one boy-sun left, Huo Yi reached for his last arrow, but his quiver was empty. Although the people were cheering him, Huo Yi lowered his bow, leaving one sun to light Earth.

When at last Earth was safe, Huo Yi rested from his labors and returned to heaven. But the King Father of the East was furious.

"I told you to frighten my sons, not kill them!" the King Father thundered. "I can never forgive you for this! Since you love humans so much, you can live with them!"

Thus Huo Yi and his wife, Chang'e (chahng uh), were turned out of heaven and stripped of their ability to live forever. During his life on Earth, Huo Yi taught other humans how to use the bow so the art would not be lost after his death. Huo Yi is still remembered for his great deeds, and so in that way, he became immortal again.

The World of HUO YI THE ARCHER

The Chinese call their country *Zhongguo*, which means *Middle Country*. This name probably came from the ancient Chinese belief that their country was the geographical center of the world and the most cultured civilization. The English name *China* probably came from *Qin* (chihn), the name of an early Chinese *dynasty* (series of rulers from the same family).

The Huang He (hwahng hu), which means *Yellow River*, flows along farmland in China's Qinghai province. China was one of the world's centers of *domestication* (regions where people began to cultivate what had been wild plants and animals). People in China were growing millet (a grain) and rice by roughly 8000 B.C. They were among the first to domesticate pigs and chickens. From China, agriculture spread to other areas of Asia.

CULTURE HEROES

Beings such as Huo Yi (how yee) who bring culture to Earth are common character types in world myths. These figures don't create the world, but they make it fit for human habitation. They give a people inventions, technology, foods, or cultural practices. Sometimes they rid the land of dangerous beasts or harmful forces. Huo Yi makes China safe for humans and teaches them the use of the bow. In some stories, he is divine and in others he is human.

The Qianlong (chee EHN loong) Emperor, who reigned in the mid-1700's, poses in his ceremonial armor while carrying a quiver of arrows, in a painting made on silk during his lifetime. Chinese artists began painting on silk more than 2,000 years ago. Most early Chinese art reflected the power and mystery of nature. But around 200 B.C., Chinese art and literature began to focus on mythical and historical figures, and human situations and values.

Early China had many towns that acted as busy market centers for agricultural produce and other goods. The Chinese were among the first peoples to use metal coins as money.

HUO YI SEEKS IMMORTALITY

When Huo Yi followed a dragon to the palace of the Queen Mother of the West, he was offered a magical drink that would make him and his wife immortal—but things did not work out that way.

In the days of Emperor Yao (yow), the third daughter of the Queen Mother of the West rode each night on a dragon to visit her mother atop sacred Kunlun (koon loon) Mountain. As it traveled, the dragon left a luminous trail in the air. Seeing this shining track, Emperor Yao sent Huo Yi (how yee), the Divine Archer, to investigate.

For many days, Huo Yi followed the dragon's trail until he came to Kunlun Mountain, which was protected by a fierce *deity* (divine being). The deity sent many winged terrors to destroy Huo Yi, but he turned them back with a single arrow. Suddenly, a door opened in the mountain and everything became still. The Queen Mother of the West emerged, followed by 10 ladies in waiting.

Recognizing the goddess, Huo Yi bowed low, introducing himself and his mission. "Greetings, Golden Mother of the Shining Lake. My master, Emperor Yao, sent me to find the cause of the shining tracks in the sky."

19

"Huo Yi is most welcome. Please enter my palace and refresh yourself," the goddess said.

Huo Yi was dazzled. The palace perched on towering jade cliffs. Trees and plants of precious gems sparkled by sunlight and twinkled by moonlight. Peach trees grew among the rocks, each bearing a fruit of immortality every 3,000 years.

The Queen Mother of the West entertained Huo Yi like a king. As the archer prepared to depart, she asked him to choose a gift. "I have heard, Golden Mother, that you have an elixir of immortality. May I take two doses?" asked Yi.

Queen Mother of the West agreed. "My attendants distill an elixir from the Peaches of Immortality that bestows eternal life. Build me a summer palace and the gift is yours." So Huo Yi built a palace on White Jade Tortoise Mountain with the help of the mountain spirits. It had 16 buildings with walls of jade, fragrant-wood beams, and a glass roof.

The Queen Mother was delighted and gave Yi the elixir of immortality. She warned him, "You must wait 12 months or the elixir will do nothing."

When Huo Yi got home, he hid the elixir in the rafters of his house. Soon after, Emperor Yao sent a message to Huo Yi: "The land is under attack. Our people perish! Defend them with your bow." Huo Yi set out at once with the emperor's soldiers. For nearly a year, they fought with wild animals, dragons, and a fierce giant named Chisel-tooth.

Meanwhile, Huo Yi's wife, Chang'e (chahng uh), sat at home, overcome with boredom. One night, she saw a faint glow on the ceiling. Curious, she climbed a ladder and found the doses of elixir hidden in the rafters. Just as she did so, she heard Huo Yi returning. Panicking, Chang'e drank both doses of the elixir. She began to float.

Huo Yi was furious. "I brought back two doses so we could live together forever on Earth!" he shouted. Frightened by her husband's fury, Chang'e jumped from a window to escape and began to float upward. Huo Yi aimed his bow, thinking at first to prevent his wife's rising by shooting at her. But he could not bear to hurt her.

Chang'e floated away until she was lost to sight. She came to rest on the moon, where she remains to this day.

The World of WARRING STATES

During the second half of the Zhou (joh) dynasty (1045 to 256 B.C.), China was troubled by conflict among the many states in the country. (A dynasty is a series of rulers from the same family.) In 476 B.C., China entered a time of almost constant war called the Warring States Period. After the Zhou dynasty ended, the scale of warfare increased as seven major states fought each other for control of the country. Finally in 221 B.C., the Qin (chihn) state, under the leadership of Shi Huangdi (shihr hwahng dee), won over the other states. Proclaiming himself the first Chinese emperor, Shi Huangdi swiftly abolished local states and established a strong central government.

Most of the Great Wall of China dates from the Ming dynasty (A.D. 1368-1644). However, the Chinese began building walls along their borders as early as the 400's B.C., during the Warring States Period. The Qin Emperor Shi Huangdi is traditionally regarded as the first ruler to conceive of, and build, a great wall.

XI WANGMU

Xi Wangmu (shee wahn moo), the Queen Mother of the West, is among the oldest *deities* (gods) in China. She was believed to live atop the mythical Kunlun (koon loon) Mountain, which connected heaven and Earth. According to Chinese mythology, the Queen Mother of the West controlled the cosmic forces of time and space. She also had power over life, death, disease, and healing and could determine the lifespan of all living beings.

IDEALIZED HEROES

Given the fierce wars leading to the unification of China, it is no surprise that the "military romance" (an idealized tale about wars and heroes) became an important story form in China. The hero of these stories, like Huo Yi (how yee), the Divine Archer, is, of course, skilled in the martial arts. But he is also supernaturally good. Often, the stories contain at least some historical truth, though the difficulties facing the hero and the wickedness of his foes are greatly exaggerated. Despite this, the warriors in these stories seem like real people whom one could try to imitate.

Wax figures re-create the teacher and students in a classroom attached to a temple in Fuzhou, China, which was devoted to Confucius (kuhn FYOO shuhs) (above left) and his philosophy. Confucius, who lived from 551? to 479? B.C., developed his philosophy in response to the conflict wracking China. Rapid political change was altering the structure of Chinese society, and many people no longer respected the traditional standards of social behavior. Confucius feared that this threat to orderly social relationships would lead to the destruction of civilization. Confucius believed that society could be saved if it emphasized moral self-cultivation in personal and public conduct, including a respect for rightful authority—both one's elders and the state—and generosity and humaneness toward others.

HUO YI AND THE PALACE OF THE SUN

After Chang'e drank the magic elixir and went to the moon, Huo Yi finally gained his own chance for immortality.

One day, not long after Chang'e (chahng uh), the wife of Huo Yi (how yee), the Divine Archer, floated to the moon, a powerful wind swept Huo Yi to the Cloud Palace of Di Jun (dee joon), the King Father of the East.

"Huo Yi," said the King Father. "Do not be angry with your wife, Chang'e, for taking your portion of the elixir of immortality. She is now an immortal in the Palace of the Moon and will be so forever. Your great and selfless deeds have earned you a similar fate. You will live as an immortal in the Palace of the Sun."

The King Father of the East ordered his servants to bake Huo Yi a cake made with oil from the sarsaparilla plant and provide him with a moon charm.

"Eat this cake, Huo Yi," said the King Father. "It will protect you from the heat of the Palace of the Sun. The charm will permit you to visit Chang'e on the moon whenever you wish."

Huo Yi ate the cake as instructed and placed the charm on his body. He thanked the King Father and started to leave.

"Wait, Huo Yi," said the King Father. "You have yet to learn the laws of day and night, the fixed times of the sun's rising and setting. Take with you the Bird of Golden Plumage whose song announces these times."

"How will I know which bird this is?" Huo Yi asked.

"This is an easy matter," replied the King Father of the East. "The Bird of Golden Plumage has three feet and has eaten of the sun's yang spirit. It lives in the great mulberry tree near a spring on an island in the Eastern Sea. It is from this spring that the sun rises at dawn. To keep the bird's call from shaking the heavens, I have ordered Intelligent Pearl, the Great Sage, to keep the bird in a cage on Peach-Blossom Hill. Fetch it from there."

The King Father of the East wrote Huo Yi a charm that would cause Intelligent Pearl to open the cage.

Huo Yi traveled to the island in the Eastern Sea where Intelligent Pearl lived. There, Huo Yi gave the charm to the Great Sage, who opened the cage of the Bird of Golden Plumage.

"This bird," said Intelligent Pearl, "lays eggs from which hatch nestlings with red combs on their heads. Every morning and night, when the Golden Bird calls out, her nestlings answer, signaling when it is time for humanity to begin and end its daily labors."

Huo Yi traveled the heavens, riding on the back of the Bird with Golden Plumage, reaching the sun's highest point at midday. Huo Yi entered the Palace of the Sun and enjoyed complete happiness. His new life was carefree and peaceful.

But one day, Huo Yi remembered the good times he had enjoyed with Chang'e and desired to see her again. Desire became reality after Huo Yi rode a sunbeam to the moon. The moon was forested with cinnamon trees and whitened with frost. In a lonely spot, he found Chang'e standing by herself.

When she saw her husband, Chang'e feared he might still be angry. But Huo Yi spoke to her gently. "Let us forget the past," he said. "I now live in the Palace of the Sun and can visit you at any time."

Huo Yi saw that his wife had no home. So he cut down many cinnamon trees and shaped many precious gems and built his wife the Palace of Great Cold. Ever after, he visited Chang'e on the 15th day of every month. At that time, Huo Yi's mighty *yang* energy combines with Chang'e's strong *yin* energy to create the full moon.

The World of the
CHINESE ZODIAC

The Chinese zodiac was said to have been started by Huangdi (hwahng dee), the Yellow Emperor, considered the ancestor of all Han Chinese, in 2,600 B.C. Ever since, the zodiac has been used to divide the passage of time into cycles of 12 years. The zodiac follows the lunar year, meaning it is based on the waxing and waning of the moon. Each year is represented by an animal, such as the rat, the snake, and the dragon. People who are born in the year of a particular animal are thought to have some of the animal's qualities. Many people still use the zodiac to predict the future and even to choose a husband or wife. Many Chinese myths and folktales represent various elements of the astrological system.

The moon plays an important role in Chinese culture. The moon is celebrated as a symbol of peace and prosperity every year during the Mid-Autumn Festival, which is held at the full moon in the eighth month of the Chinese calendar (September or October in the Western calendar). The festival began as a celebration of the end of the harvest. People try to return home from wherever they are in China to watch the full moon and eat mooncakes, round pastries filled with bean paste.

鳳凰 日

The Bird of Golden Plumage resembles the mythical phoenix, a bird that lived for many years, burned itself in a fire, and rose new from the ashes. Images of a magical bird that brought good luck date to 8,000 B.C. in China. Early accounts describe the bird as having a rooster's beak, a swallow's head, a serpent's neck, a tortoise's humped back, and the tail of a fish. The bird is sometimes depicted as having three legs. Later stories associated the bird's six key features with the six celestial points: sky (head), sun (eyes), moon (back), wind (wings), Earth (the feet), and the planets (tail). The phoenix is said to appear only in areas of peace and prosperity.

Chinese dragon dancers celebrate the New Year in Foshan City. The dragon dance is traditionally performed at New Year to scare away evil spirits. The dancers use poles to raise and lower the dragon's head and body. The dragons can be up to 330 feet (100 meters) long. Longer dragons are thought to be luckier than shorter ones.

HUO YI, A SOLAR DEITY

In a country as ancient and multiethnic as China, myths have many variations. In an early tradition, Huo Yi (how yee), the Divine Archer, is depicted as the champion of archery and a brave warrior. In the later Taoist tradition, Huo Yi is an architect, a solar deity, and the embodiment of *yang*, the male principle of light, action, and air. Taoist influences explain why in one story, the King Father of the East despises Yi for killing 9 of his 10 sons and curses him to a mortal life on Earth, while in another story the King Father grants Huo Yi immortality. Taoist influences also explain why the relationship between male and female, sun and moon, and yang and yin are emphasized in all the stories of Huo Yi.

YU TAMES THE FLOOD

When Yu set out to protect China from terrible floods, he used his great energy and engineering skills—but also some divine help.

During the reign of Emperor Yao (yow), a great flood swept over the land. The waters covered the land for more than a generation, filling the Huang He (hwahng hu) and Yangtze (yahng dzuh) river valleys and causing famine among the people. Yao consulted with the spirits of the Four Mountains, who advised him to instruct Gun, Prince of Chong, to end the flood. Yao was reluctant to follow the advice because he knew Gun was dishonest and tricky.

Nevertheless, Yao did as the spirits had advised and appointed Gun to put an end to the flood.

Gun surveyed the flooded valleys where the waters seemed to boil up to the very sky. This gave Gun an idea. He crept into heaven and stole the magical self-expanding soil of Tai Di (ty dee), the highest god. Tai Di was furious, but even so, Gun managed to return to Earth with his ill-gotten treasure.

Gun placed the magical soil here and there to create earthworks and dams to control the surging waters. But even after nine years, the floodwaters had not receded. The people's suffering increased. Gun's dikes and dams began to collapse.

Ashamed that Gun, whom he had chosen for the task, had failed to control the vast flood, Emperor Yao offered to resign his office to the spirits of the Four Mountains. The spirits suggested that Yao name Shun, a distant relative, as his replacement. Again, the emperor had doubts about the spirits' advice because Shun was not accustomed to court life. Yao devised a series of tests for Shun, but Shun proved both clever and strong. And so, Shun eventually replaced Yao.

When Shun became emperor, he sought to restore order by dividing the people among four islands. Shun visited the four remaining corners of his flooded land, meeting with the leaders in each place.

The new emperor created a new calendar, standardized weights and measures, and decreed many other rules and procedures to create stability and a sense of common purpose among his scattered people. Meanwhile, Gun worked even harder to control the flood, compelling armies of laborers to build the dikes and dams higher than ever. But Gun's efforts failed once again. Shun banished Gun to Feather Mountain.

Emperor Shun finally appointed Gun's son, Yu (yoo), to control the floods. Yu was the opposite of his father. He was reverent, diligent, honest, and selfless. Yu worked tirelessly. He marked trees and rocks to establish boundaries and plot out channels. He never stayed a night in his own house, even when he passed by his own gate. For 13 years, Yu let his own property go to waste while he labored to restore the lands the floods had swallowed.

Once he understood the layout of the land, Yu dug canals to lead the waters toward the sea. Unfortunately, the path was blocked by the Wushan (woo shan) Mountains. Yu tried to cut a pass, but the rock was as hard as iron. The flood waters crashed into the mountains, and many of Yu's workers died. After months, Yu despaired that he had made no progress.

Yao Ji (yow jee), the 23rd daughter of the Queen Mother of the West, was moved by Yu's struggles. She was saddened by the sufferings of the people on Earth, so she decided to help. She advised Yu to use fire to burn a pass through the mountains. She sent four divine generals from Heaven to help in the task.

With their help, Yu commanded his workers to light fires at both ends of the mountain. At the same time, Yao Ji and the four generals threw thunderbolts at the cliffs. This went on for 49 days. Then the fires and thunderbolts began to have an effect—the rock softened. Yu's workers managed to dig a pass through the Wushan Mountains and the flood water passed to the sea. After the flood subsided, Wushan became the three beautiful gorges of the Yangtze River.

But building the pass had used up all of Yao Ji's divine energy. She could not return to Heaven, so she remained on Earth and turned into a mountain peak named "Goddess Peak." The celestial handmaidens who always accompanied her turned into Wushan's 12 mountain peaks.

The World of **YU**

According to Chinese tradition, Yu (yoo) the Great (right) ruled China from 2070 to 2061 B.C. and founded the Xia (shee ah) culture. For many years, experts doubted that the Xia really existed. But archaeologists found evidence of this culture in what is now Henan province. Some scholars consider the Xia culture China's first *dynasty* (family of rulers). However, most scholars consider the Shang (shahng) dynasty, which ruled from about 1766 B.C. to about 1045 B.C., the earliest known Chinese dynasty because it is known from historical records.

THE YELLOW RIVER

Throughout China's history, the Huang He (hwahng hu) has been both a blessing and a curse for the Chinese. The Huang He (Yellow River) deposits fertile *silt* (particles of soil) on the land along the river, but it has also been responsible for a number of devastating natural disasters. The worst Huang He flood occurred in 1887, when the river overflowed an area of about 50,000 square miles (130,000 square kilometers). Nearly a million people died in this flood. From 500,000 to 6 million others died from starvation and disease after the flood.

The Huang He got its name from the large amounts of soft yellow earth it carries. This silt is deposited in such large amounts at the river's bottom that it raises the bed above the surrounding plain and causes the river to change its course often. If the river floods, the water may burst its banks, covering the plains. The Chinese have maintained dikes and dams for hundreds of years to lessen the danger, but the river has never been completely controlled.

China's longest river is the Yangtze (yahng dzuh), which runs roughly parallel to the Huang He in the southern part of the country. The Yangtze is also the longest river in Asia. Like the Huang He river valley, the Yangtze's fertile valley encouraged the development of civilization. The Yangtze is also navigable along much of its length, so it became a major trade route into the heart of China.

Barges float through the city of Suzhou (soo joh) on the Grand Canal, one of the greatest achievements of Chinese engineering. The canal, which is the world's longest artificial river, extends some 1,103 miles (1,776 kilometers) and connects the cities of Beijing (bay jihng) and Hangzhou (hahng joh). Construction of the canal began during the Zhou (joh) dynasty (1045-281 B.C.). During the Sui (sway) dynasty (A.D. 581-618), a number of rivers and existing canals were connected. The Sui emperor wanted to make it easier to transport grain from the fertile basin of the Yangtze to the empire's political and military center in the north.

HOW LIN MO NIANG
Became Goddess of the Sea

The Chinese told this story to explain
how an unusual child became the
protector of those who sail the seas.

The Lin family were fishers who lived on Meizhou (may joh), an island near Taiwan. They had five sons and one daughter. Mrs. Lin wanted another daughter. She prayed to Kuan Yin (kwahn yihn), goddess of compassion, to help her. She was so earnest in her prayers that one night the goddess appeared to her in a dream. "Take this lotus blossom and eat it," said Kuan Yin. Mrs. Lin did so and became pregnant that very night. Nine months later she had a baby daughter, just as she hoped. She named the baby Lin Niang (LEEN NEE ahng).

It was clear at once that Niang was no ordinary baby. When she was born, the room was filled with the aroma of flowers. Even more remarkable, Lin Niang never cried once, not even when she was born. So her family called her Mo, which means *silent*.

Lin Mo remained just as unusual as she grew up. When she was aged only four, Kuan Yin gave her "second sight." The goddess's gift was like a special sense. It allowed Lin Mo to know about events that had not yet happened. She saw these future events in dreams or trances.

When Lin Mo was 13, a Buddhist priest noticed that she had extraordinary gifts.

He took her on as a student. For years, Lin Mo studied with him, growing more compassionate and learning how to use her spiritual gifts. She also learned martial arts.

One day when Lin Mo was 15, she went with her friends to try on new dresses. They stood by the still sea to admire their reflections. All at once a fierce dragon burst from the depths with a bronze coin in its mouth. Lin Mo's friends ran away screaming, but she remained calm. The towering beast leaned down and offered the coin to Lin Mo. She took it, and from that day on, she possessed miraculous powers. She became a healer. She could also predict the weather and often used her powers to warn Meizhou's fishers when she foresaw storms.

Compassion is beautiful and necessary, but it is also costly, especially for someone with second sight. By the time she was 19, Lin Mo's dreams and trances had shown her many tragedies at sea. Each one broke her heart. Nothing, however, so crushed her spirit as the day a towering wave struck Meizhou, sweeping away 100 villagers. For weeks, Lin Mo was too sad to leave her room. She lay on her side in her bed, facing the

wall, taking no interest in food, drink, or the outside world.

One night, Lin Mo heard a horse whinny. A horse! On Meizhou! Such a thing was impossible. Fishers don't need horses, and so there were none on the island. None living, that is. There was only an iron statue of a horse on a pedestal that had been erected in the village square to honor a nobleman. But Lin Mo dismissed this strange event and gave in to illness once more.

The next night, she again heard a horse. This was too strange! Her curiosity aroused, Lin Mo forced herself from her bed and looked out the window. But she could not see any horses. She became so curious that the next night she dressed and waited, determined to find the source of this impossible whinnying.

When she heard a horse this time, she ran outside, looking everywhere. The only horse anywhere was the iron statue in the village square. Lin Mo touched the statue, and the iron horse became flesh and blood, snorting and pawing the ground! She put her arms around the horse's neck, climbed on its back—and they were off like a lightning flash! After that, she could ride swiftly across the waves to rescue those in peril. Then she would return the horse to its pedestal, and it would resume its iron form.

One day, Lin Mo sat at a loom weaving. She fell into a trance and saw her father and brother swept overboard in a storm. She used her powers to travel in spirit form to the scene, wearing the red dress and scarf she always wore when warning others of disaster or rescuing them.

Lin Mo grabbed her brother and brought him safely home. In a blink, she returned to grab her father from the waves. But Lin Mo's mother, seeing her daughter nodding at the loom, touched her to see if she was all right. This woke Lin Mo from her trance, and she dropped her father, who drowned. Lin Mo walked across the waves to find her father's

Lin Mo died when she was only 28 years old. One day, while working with her mother, she said, "I must go now." Without another word, she walked out the door, out of the village, and to the top of Meizhou's mountain. A rainbow appeared—announcing the presence of a dragon and good fortune. Lin Mo was covered by clouds and taken to heaven.

In our days, we speak of Lin Mo as Mazu (mah tsoo), the Sea Goddess. Sailors from our country and others hereabouts pray to Mazu before beginning a voyage and give her thanks upon their safe return. Many sailors tell stories of seeing a woman in red who warns them of a coming storm or a rocky shore. She is

The World of LIN MO NIANG

China has more than 9,000 miles (14,500 kilometers) of coastline, and fish have always been central to the Chinese diet. Fishing is so important to Chinese culture that the words for *abundance* and *fish* sound the same—"yu"—and fish and fishing feature in many early myths. Fu Xi (foo shee), the god credited by some myths with creating humans, taught people to fish.

This temple to Mazu stands on Meizhou (may joh) Island, where Lin Mo is said to have lived. Like other Chinese temples, the building takes the form of a pagoda, or tower. Each story in the tower is smaller than the one beneath it. The shape is based on that of Buddhist monuments that originated in India but spread to China. One special Chinese feature is the turned-up corners of the roof. The corners help reduce the weight the overhang places on the rest of the building.

In Chinese folklore, dragons like the ones that gave Lin Mo the special coin are closely related to koi (koy) carp. These brightly colored fish have large scales that resemble the scales of a dragon. Some people say that a carp will be transformed into a dragon if it leaps up the falls of the Huang He (hwahng hu). Koi carp themselves are considered symbolic. The fish represents the power of the life force and the ability to overcome obstacles. It is also seen as a symbol of good luck, prosperity, and long life. Today koi are widely kept in ornamental ponds. The most beautiful examples are worth huge sums of money.

LIN MO NIANG

Lin Mo Niang (LEEN moh NEE ahng) is a patron and goddess of seafarers. She was also an actual person. Born in the city of Putian (POO tyehn) in Fujian (FOO jyon) province, she is first mentioned in records from the Song dynasty (A.D. 960–1279). The legendary deeds and wonders attributed to her indicate that she was an extraordinary woman. In keeping with Buddhist practice at the time, "Silent Maiden Lin" was *deified* (made a god) after her death. Today, she is known as Mazu (mah tsoo) or Ma-Tsu, the Goddess of the Sea. Her most important temples are located in Putian and on the island of Taiwan.

According to Chinese mythology, Fu Xi taught people how to fish. At first, Fu Xi fished with his hands. But after watching a spider, he learned to weave threads into nets. He taught net making to his children. Today, Chinese fishers still use nets. Some also use cormorants, birds that catch fish by diving underwater, to retrieve fish from lakes and rivers. Rings around the birds' throat prevent them from swallowing the fish.

A fisher wearing clothing common among the Huian people in China's Fujian province mends her fishing net.

BODHIDHARMA
Comes to China

The monk Bodhidharma is perhaps best remembered for introducing tea to China, but that was only a small part of his influential teachings and his long and complicated story.

Once an Indian prince named Bodhitara (BOH dee TAHR uh) became a Buddhist priest after studying for years. When his teacher died, the priest decided to go to China. Bodhidharma (BOH dee DAHR muh), as the priest was now known, stood out among the Chinese. He was dark-skinned, had a bushy beard, and wore rough clothes. People called him "the blue-eyed barbarian."

Eventually word of the strange foreigner reached Emperor Wu. The Emperor was a Buddhist who had followed Buddhist teaching by paying for the building and upkeep of temples, banning the sacrifice of animals, and forbidding the execution of criminals. The Emperor summoned Bodhidharma to his palace to meet him and see what all the fuss was about.

"Bodhidharma," Wu said, "perhaps you have heard of the many temples and priests I have supported for the good of the Buddhist way? How much merit would you say these works have earned me?" "None," replied Bodhidharma.

The Emperor was shocked! While he encouraged his counselors to speak their minds, no one ever spoke so bluntly to him! "Who are you to speak to me this way?" he demanded. "I don't know," said Bodhidharma. This enraged the Emperor. "Get out of my sight!" he said. So Bodhidharma smiled, bowed, and left without saying a word.

One day, Bodhidharma went to hear a famous priest named Shen Guang (shehn gong). Shen Guang had been a fierce general but had given up his life of violence to become a Buddhist priest. As Shen preached, Bodhidharma occasionally nodded his head in agreement; more often, he would shake his head in disagreement. Shen Guang was angry that this odd-looking foreigner disagreed with him in front of his followers. He tore the meditation beads from his neck and threw them at Bodhidharma. The beads knocked out Bodhidharma's two front teeth, but he smiled, turned, and walked away without a word.

Shen Guang was fascinated, so he followed Bodhidharma for days, then weeks, as the strange man walked from the Southern Kingdom to the Wei (way) Mountains in the north. Eventually they came to the Yangtze (yahng dzuh) River. Bodhidharma sat down next to an elderly woman with a pile of reeds.

"Greetings, mother," said Bodhidharma, "Would you give me one of your reeds?" "Certainly, sir," she replied. Setting the reed on the river, Bodhidharma stepped on it and, through his great power, propelled himself across the river. Seeing this miracle, Shen Guang ran up to the woman, took an armful of reeds, and tossed them in the river. When he stepped on them, he sank to the bottom and began to drown. The old woman rescued him.

Spluttering on shore, Shen Guang asked, "Why could I not ride across the river like that blue-eyed barbarian?" "Because you disrespected me by taking my reeds without permission and in disrespecting me, you disrespected yourself. You seek a master, Shen Guang, and the foreigner you follow is that master." Moments later, the former general found himself propelled across the Yangtze.

Eventually, Bodhidharma came to the Shaolin (show leen) Monastery. He stood outside the gate. The abbot came to greet him. "Who are you, foreigner?" asked the abbot. "What do you seek?" Bodhidharma made no answer. "I asked you a question," the abbot said. "If you wish lodging for the night, you'd better learn manners!"

When Bodhidharma still did not reply, the abbot sent him away. Bodhidharma walked up a hill and entered a cave to meditate. He stayed there with his face turned to the wall for the nine years!

Shen Guang took it upon himself to protect Bodhidharma. From time to time, he begged Bodhidharma to be his teacher, but Bodhidharma was silent.

One night during a snowstorm, Shen Guang lost patience. He hurled a block of snow into Bodhidharma's cave. "When will you agree to be my teacher?!" he shouted. Bodhidharma turned around and spoke. "When red snow falls," he said.

Shen Guang rushed from the cave, grabbed his old sword, and cut off his own arm. He waved the severed limb in the air, spattering the snow with his blood. He then threw his arm into the cave. "Here, teacher, the snow is red!"

Bodhidharma turned again and said, "You may be my student. Your priestly name is Dazu Huike (DAH zoo HWAY kuh)." Dazu Huike realized that Bodhidharma's teaching did not take the form of words.

Eventually, many students gathered around Bodhidharma. They learned to face the wall and meditate. Often the Master's students nodded off on their cushions. To help them stay alert, the Master plucked off his eyelids and threw them on the ground. Overnight, they became tea plants. Bodhidharma took the leaves, brewed them in boiling water, and taught his students to drink the beverage to keep them alert during periods of meditation.

When he was 150 years old, Bodhidharma gathered his students around him. "My death approaches," he announced. "Please demonstrate your understanding of the teaching."

A student named Dao Fu (dow foo) approached and said, "It is not bound by words and phrases, nor is it separate from words and phrases. This is the function of the Tao (dow)." "You have attained my skin," replied Bodhidharma.

Zong Chi (zawhng jih), a nun, approached and said, "It is like a glimpse of the glorious Buddha-land. Seen once, it need not be seen again." "You have attained my flesh," replied Bodhidharma.

Dao Fu approached once more and said, "The four elements are empty. The five senses are without existence. Not one law that governs the universe—no, not one dharma (DAHR muh)—can be understood." "You have attained my bones," replied Bodhidharma.

At last, one-armed Dazu Huike approached, bowed deeply, and said nothing. "You have attained my marrow," said the Master. "Accept now my robe and bowl for you must replace me."

45

The World of BODHIDHARMA

Buddhism reached China from India before A.D. 100, during the Later Han *dynasty* (series of family rulers), which lasted from A.D. 25 to 220. Buddhism became well established throughout the country during the 300's. The religion's focus on seeking truth behind the appearance of reality clashed with Confucianism, which the Han had made the state philosophy. After the Han dynasty fell, many of the ruling elite turned to Buddhism. Under the influence of Taoism (TOW ihz uhm), a Chinese religious and philosophical tradition, several *schools* (types) of Buddhism developed in China. Bodhidharma's (BOH dee DAHR muhz) focus on silent meditation and actions that reveal enlightenment was the basis of a movement known in China as Ch'an Buddhism. The school migrated to Japan, and is now known in western countries as Zen Buddhism.

Ch'an Buddhist nuns pray above a giant staute of the Buddha at a monastery in China's Sichuan (SEHCH won) province.

The mountainous landscape Bodhidharma found in China has inspired artists and such calligraphers as Mao Yinfu (mow yihn foo) (left), for thousands of years. (Calligraphy is the art of beautiful handwriting.) For Chinese artists, painting with a brush and ink is a spiritual experience. Instead of painting places in a realistic way, they concentrate on making deliberate strokes with the brush. Following the traditional rules of such painting enables artists to achieve deep levels of concentration and self-expression.

TEA

Tea is an essential beverage in China. It is drunk throughout the day as a substitute for water. For centuries, people believed that tea possessed healing qualities and used it in folk medicines. Scientists now know that tea contains chemical substances called antioxidants, which may prevent some types of damage to the cells of the body. Other legends besides the story of Bodhidharma explain the origin of tea. In one story, an ancient emperor preferred drinking boiled water. One day some wild tea leaves fell into the water, and the fragrance enticed the emperor to taste it. He liked it— and soon everyone was drinking tea.

Women perform a traditional tea ceremony in Yixing, Jiangsu Province, China. Tea drinking was raised to an art form in China, where it was intended to improve relations among people, bless ceremonies, and encourage people to express themselves through the arts. Formal tea ceremonies are designed to demonstrate respect for the one served through the server's grace and perfect *etiquette* (manners). Tea ceremonies highlight the importance of cherishing beauty in an imperfect world.

HUANGDI

and the Realm of Hua-Hsu

The Emperor Huangdi brought stability to China during a time of war. He became lazy, however, and neglected his duties until he visited a divine kingdom in a dream.

In the earliest times, there was war in heaven. Demons shattered the pillars of heaven, causing devastating floods and fires. The only survivors were one man, Fu Xi (foo shee), and one woman, Nüwa (noo WAH), a brother and sister. They washed ashore on Kunlun (koon loon) Mountain. They prayed to Shangdi (shahng dee), the Highest Lord, for the power to create people.

Nüwa was blessed in this way: She made figurines of yellow clay and gave them life and the power to create more beings. Over time, Earth again had many people. Nüwa also replaced the pillars of heaven by melting and shaping five colored stones into new pillars. In these ways, order was restored in heaven and on Earth.

For his part, Fu Xi organized the growing number of people. He taught them the art of fishing with nets, the cooking of food, and iron making. Fu Xi also created the idea and practice of marriage and taught the people to thank the gods and goddesses by offering up gifts to them.

One day, while sitting by the River Luo (loh), a turtle emerged from the river. On its back were trigrams, marks with three lines of different lengths. Fu Xi cut the marks on bones and created the I Ching (ee jihng), a way to predict one's fortune.

By the time Fu Xi and Nüwa became immortals and went to heaven, there were millions of people on Earth. But the land was torn by war as groups of people fought. In the chaos, Huangdi (hwahng dee), the Yellow Emperor, through courage and intelligence, calmed the warring groups and brought stability.

The people flourished and prospered. Huangdi himself, having accomplished so much good, began to relax. He enjoyed food, drink, and entertainment in abundance every day. Over time, his senses became dull. He was no longer energetic and often seemed less interested in attending to the responsibilities of his office than feasting and drinking.

The kingdom began to fail much like the Yellow Emperor's body. One night, Huangdi dreamed he had flown to the realm of Hua-Hsu (hwah shoo), mother of the great Fu Xi who helped restore order after the destruction of the heavenly pillars. In the realm of Hua-Hsu, there was no ruler. The people governed themselves. They were not driven by cravings and selfishness. They followed their natural instincts. They enjoyed life but did not fear death. In their deep serenity, they could walk on air as though it were the land. Beauty and ugliness did not break their hearts.

When Huangdi awoke, he realized he had been living in error. A life addicted to the cravings of the senses is false!

Assembling his counselors he said, "The Tao—the Way—cannot be found through the senses. I know how to find this way, but I cannot explain it to you. You must find it for yourselves."

So he dismissed his counselors and moved to a hut in the courtyard of the palace. He ate little and drank only water and tea. Soon, he felt and looked much better. He felt energy to work again. So he began creating a perfect kingdom. By the time he died, at the age of 400, China very nearly resembled the heavenly land of Hua-Hsu.

The World of
HUANGDI

Huangdi (hwahng dee), also known as the Yellow Emperor, is a legendary figure who, according to tradition, established the Chinese civilization. He was said to have created a *utopia* (ideal society) based on virtues similar to those promoted by Taoism (TOW ihz uhm). Taoism, which is also spelled Daoism (DOW ihz uhm), emphasizes harmony with the Tao. The word *tao* originally meant road or way. However, Taoists always have thought that the Tao is hard to put into words. They often have described it as the underlying pattern of the universe, the mother of all things, and the *spontaneous* (naturally occurring) process regulating the natural cycle of the universe. The primary qualities Taoism encourages are naturalness, simplicity, humility, spontaneity, and moderation. Taoism values *wu wei* (woo way)—"action without effort." Individuals are encouraged to accept each moment as it is rather than imposing on it their ideas about how things should or could be.

Laozi (low zee) (left), who wrote one of the basic books of Taoism, appears with Confucius and the young Buddha, in a painting from the Qing dynasty (A.D. 1644 to 1912).

UTOPIAS

Utopias are ideal societies. Many writers have used the idea of a utopia as a way to criticize the world in which they live. The world's myths feature many stories of lands where people do not fight, steal, or kill, and where they live extraordinarily long and healthy lives because they embody virtues. In the story "Huangdi and the Realm of Hua-Hsu," Huangdi experiences the utopian realm of Hua-Hsu where everyone embodies the virtues enshrined in the teachings of Taoism.

A Taoist monk in Shandong performs tai chi (TY JEE), a method of exercise and self-protection based on careful movements and spiritual discipline.

Ladies of the Chinese court prepare a length of newly woven silk fabric for sewing by ironing it with a device containing hot coals. The fire for heating the coals sits behind them. Silk is made from the cocoons of caterpillars called silkworms. According to a Chinese legend, silk was discovered about 2700 B.C. in the garden of Emperor Huangdi. The emperor ordered his wife to find out what was damaging his mulberry trees. She found white worms eating the mulberry leaves and spinning shiny cocoons. She accidentally dropped a cocoon into hot water. As she played with the cocoon in the water, a delicate, cobwebby tangle separated itself from the cocoon. She drew it out and found that one slender thread was unwinding itself from the cocoon. She had discovered silk.

I CHING

The I Ching (ee jihng) is a book that was originally used to predict the future. It is the earliest and most important book of the ancient Chinese texts called the *Five Classics*. It is also known as the *Book of Changes*. The I Ching probably originated early in the Zhou dynasty (about 1045-256 B.C.). By the 500's B.C., the I Ching had become a book of philosophy. The Chinese philosopher Confucius taught the I Ching as a book of moral wisdom.

According to Chinese tradition, Huangdi, the Yellow Emperor, ruled during the 2600's B.C. He is credited with introducing farming, writing, the bow and arrow, boats, coined money, astronomy, wooden carts, and many other useful devices to China. Many Chinese families trace their ancestry to Huangdi.

JOURNEY TO THE WEST

The ambitions of Sunwukong, the Monkey King, led him into war against the Jade Emperor. Centuries later, after he had been severely punished, Sunwukong set out on an epic journey.

Sunwukong (suhn woo kohng), the Monkey King, was extraordinarily intelligent and able, but he was mischievous, too, and tended to act wildly. He learned magic tricks from a Taoist master and could assume the shape of 72 different things. If need be, Monkey King could become as small as a flea or as large as an elephant. There was no enemy he could not destroy.

Sunwukong wanted to be immortal, so he sought to become a great king. In time, his schemes brought him face to face with the Jade Emperor, the ruler of heaven, Earth, and the underworld. "Do not call yourself king, Monkey,"

commanded the Jade Emperor. "I am a king, and I will be immortal one day," Sunwukong shouted.

The Jade Emperor sent armies from heaven to destroy Monkey, but in battle after battle, Monkey outwitted them. Eventually, members of the Jade Emperor's court suggested he should consider the cost of the war and make peace. So the Jade Emperor offered Monkey an official title. But Monkey was furious to discover that he had been named the cleaner of the heavenly stables and everyone was laughing at him.

From then on, Monkey worked even harder to become king of Earth. The armies of heaven came against him, but each time, Monkey found a way to defeat or escape them. Finally, all the gods of heaven and all their followers together captured Sunwukong. The Jade Emperor sentenced the Monkey King to death. But however they tried, Monkey would not die. Monkey simply laughed and humiliated the Jade Emperor further.

Desperate, the Jade Emperor appealed to the Lord Buddha for help. The Buddha dropped the Mount of Five Fingers on Sunwukong. Although burying Monkey under the mountain did not kill him, it made it impossible for him to move.

Five hundred years later, the monk, Tripitika (trih piht uh kuh), began a difficult journey to the Western Paradise to visit Lord Buddha and retrieve a copy of the Buddhist scriptures for China. The Buddha arranged for Sunwukong and two other companions to accompany Tripitika. He released Monkey from the mountain.

At first, the struggles of Tripitika and his companions seemed too much to

bear. They climbed steep mountains and crossed burning deserts. They faced wild beasts and terrible demons—none of whom wished for Buddhism to spread to China. They fought among one another and complained bitterly.

But after several years, even Monkey began to realize that he needed his companions. He learned that cooperation and mutual respect were necessary to accomplish their task.

Monkey was brave and clever, and each time the small band was threatened, he kept them together. By the time they reached the Western Paradise 14 years later, Sunwukong had all but forgotten his lust for power and all those battles he had fought against the Jade Emperor.

The Buddha met Tripitika, Sunwukong, and their companions at the gates of the Western Paradise and gave them the scriptures. He acknowledged their great suffering, told them what they had learned about themselves and the true nature of things, and rewarded them with immortality and happiness.

The World of THE MONKEY KING

Siddhartha Gautama (sih DAHR tuh GOW tuh muh), commonly known as the Buddha (the Enlightened One) (below), founded the religion known as Buddhism. Almost no authentic information exists about the details of Buddha's life. But most scholars agree that such a man lived in northern India during the 500's and 400's B.C. Buddha's followers spread the story of his life. Buddhism, one of the world's great religions, is founded on the Four Noble Truths. The first is that suffering exists and will always exist. The second is that suffering is caused by attachment to things, people, and ideas. The third is that suffering may be relieved by letting go of our attachments. The fourth is that there is a reliable path that leads away from attachment and therefore away from suffering.

THE NOBLE PATH

The Noble Eightfold Path summarizes the attributes a Buddhist must cultivate to be freed from suffering: 1) right perception or understanding of the world; 2) right attitude or thought about the world; 3) right speech; 4) right action; 5) proper livelihood; 6) right effort; 7) right mindfulness; and 8) right meditation. What each of these eight attributes means in practical terms is something the individual must work out through meditation and study.

Xuanzang (shyoo ahn zahng) (A.D. 602–664) was an influential Buddhist monk, scholar, and traveler. Like many Buddhists of his time, Xuanzang was concerned that without a more complete collection of scriptures, Buddhism in China was incomplete and misdirected. In 626, Xuanzang set out for India, the birthplace of Buddhism, on what became a 16-year journey to collect works of Buddhist scripture. His travels were dangerous and difficult. His story was written down some 900 years after he returned to China, bearing more than 600 Buddhist texts that he then spent the rest of his life translating.

A Ch'an Buddhist monk practices kung fu at the ancient Shaolin (show leen) Monastery, in Zhengzhou (juhng joh), China. The monks at the monastery are some of the world's leading experts on the martial arts. According to tradition, the legendary Yellow Emperor, Huangdi (hwahng dee), introduced the martial arts to China in the 2500's B.C. The first historical records of martial arts in the country date to the 400's B.C. The martial arts have been viewed as important parts of a cultivated life in Confucianism, Taoism, and Buddhism.

THE MONKEY KING

Sunwukong, the Monkey King, is one of the most enduring and beloved figures in Chinese literature. He is enormously strong and supernaturally fast. He is capable of taking 72 different animal forms, but he cannot transform his monkey tail. He is able to stand up to the strongest warriors of heaven and possesses great magical power with which he can control water and wind, demons and heavenly beings, and human beings. In modern times, the Monkey King has inspired novels, plays, a television series, and the Japanese manga series *Dragon Ball*.

A scholar stands beside a horse tethered to a tree in a carving on a jade pebble. The title "Jade Emperor" given to the ruler of the heavens, Earth, and the underworld in the story of the Monkey King is a reminder of the importance of jade to the Chinese. The green stone has a *luminous* (bright) quality that the Chinese believed represented heaven. Jade is also a symbol of beauty and value. In Confucian teaching, jade stands for such virtues as courage, modesty, fairness, and compassion.

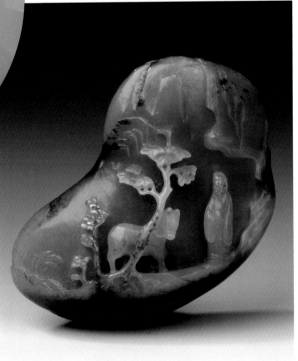

DEITIES OF CHINA

Chang'e (chahng uh)

The wife of Huo Yi, the Divine Archer, Chang'e floated to the moon and became a deity after drinking both doses of the elixir of immortality given to Huo Yi by the Queen Mother of the West. Huo Yi built a palace for his wife using cinnamon trees.

Di Jun (dee joon)

Di Jun, the King Father of the East, is the representative of yin, the male quality of yin and yang, two crucial concepts in Taoism. He is married to Xi Wangmu and is the god of immortality.

Fu Xi (foo shee)

China's mythical first emperor and the creator of humans. Born as a god with a snake's body, he is credited with having discovered the mysteries of the I Ching and taught humans essential skills.

Huangdi (hwahng dee)

Also known as the Yellow Emperor, Huangdi is a legendary figure who tradition says established the Chinese civilization. He was said to have created a *utopia* (ideal society) based on virtues similar to those later promoted by Taoism.

Huo Yi (how yee), the Divine Archer

Huo Yi was charged by the King Father of the East with stopping the 10 boy-suns from destroying Earth. But the King Father banished Huo Yi to Earth after he shot down nine of the boy-suns. On Earth he taught humans useful skills. Huo Yi, who was married to Chang'e, later became immortal and went to live in the sun.

Kuan Yin (kwahn yihn)

The goddess of compassion, Kuan Yin helped Mrs. Lin give birth to Liang Mo Niang, who became Mazu, the goddess of the sea.

Lin Mo Niang (LEEN moh NEE ahng)

During her life on Earth, Lin "the Silent" had the ability to calm storms and rescue the drowning. After her death, she was deified as Mazu, the Sea Goddess. Sailors in danger call on her for help.

Nüwa (noo WAH)

The Chinese creator-goddess, she made humans to relieve her boredom after Earth was created and originally filled only with animals. Married to Fu Xi, she also saved the world from a great flood caused by two warring gods in heaven.

P'an Ku (pahn koo)

At the beginning of everything, all the world and Pan Ku were contained in an egg, which one day cracked and split. The white floated up to form the heavens, and the yolk sank and became Earth. Pan Ku grew hugely tall, and ever since, he has been standing with the heavens on his shoulders to keep heaven and Earth apart.

Sunwukong (suhn woo kohng)

Also known as the Monkey King, Sunwukong hatched as a stone egg from a rock. The Chinese trickster god, he enraged the other gods and was subjected to a series of punishments, including being buried under a mountain for 500 years, before being forgiven.

Tai Di (ty dee)

Tai Di was the source of the universe and everything in it.

Xi Wangmu (shee wahn moo)

After offering a bowl of magic peaches to the Emperor of China, Xi Wangmu was raised from her original incarnation as tiger-spirit and plague-carrier to become the Queen Mother of the West. She became the embodiment of femininity after marrying Di Jun, the King Father of the West, who represented masculinity.

Yao Ji (yow jee)

The 23rd daughter of the Queen Mother of the West, Yao Ji helped Yu open the Wushan Pass to let the floodwaters of the Huang He (Yellow Sea) flow to the sea. But because she used up all of her divine energy to do this, she became a mountain peak named "Goddess Peak."

Yunhua, Lady (LEEN moh NEE ahng) of the Cloudy Flower

Lady Yunhua was one of the supernatural beings who helped Yu build dams and dikes to tame the Huang He (Yellow River). She lived on one of the peaks of the Wushan Mountains.

Xi Wangmu, the Queen Mother of the West

GLOSSARY

calligraphy The art of beautiful writing. In Asia, calligraphers wrote with a brush on paper, the shapes of the forms depending on the pressure and movement of the brush.

creation The process by which the universe was brought into being at the start of time.

creator god A god who creates the universe or Earth, geographical features, and often all humans or a particular culture. Creation myths often explain the origin of the world by describing actions that take place in a world that already exists.

deity A god or goddess.

dharma The eternal law of the cosmos, which is carried in the essence of all things.

dynasty A series of rulers from the same family.

elixir A substance supposed to have the power of changing lead, iron, or other metal, into gold or of lengthening life indefinitely.

enlightenment A state of freedom from earthly concerns that is the ideal goal of Buddhism and other religions.

immortality The quality of being able to live forever.

meditate To focus one's mind, usually for a religious or spiritual benefit.

myth A traditional story that explains the origins of a people or natural and social phenomena. Myths often involve gods, spirits, and other supernatural beings.

pagoda A type of tower commonly associated with Buddhist temples. In China, most pagodas have eight sides and an uneven number of stories. They are made of wood, masonry, glazed tile, or porcelain and are decorated with ivory, bone, and stonework. Originally, each element in the design of a pagoda had religious meaning.

phoenix A mythical bird that burns itself on a fire then rises again from the ashes.

qi A life-force energy that flows from living and inanimate objects.

ritual A solemn religious ceremony in which a set of actions are performed in a specific order.

sacred Something that is connected with the gods or goddesses and so should be treated with respectful worship.

sacrifice An offering made to a god or gods, often in the form of an animal or even a person who is killed for the purpose. Sacrifices also take the shape of valued possessions that might be buried, placed in caves, or thrown into a lake for the gods.

sage A person famed for being wise.

scripture The sacred texts of a religion.

silt Very fine particles of earth, sand, clay, or similar matter, carried by moving water.

supernatural Describes something that cannot be explained by science or by the laws of nature, which is therefore said to be caused by beings such as gods, spirits, or ghosts.

yang The element in Chinese philosophy representing the male qualities of light and heat.

yin The element in Chinese philosophy representing the female qualities of darkness and cold.

zodiac The division of the year or another period into equal parts, each governed by its own astrological sign.

FOR FURTHER INFORMATION

Books

Allan, Tony, and Charles Phillips. *Ancient Chinese Myths and Beliefs* (World Mythologies). Rosen Publishing Group, 2012.

Bingham, Jane. *Chinese Myths* (Myths from Many Lands). Windmill Books, 2009.

Cotterell, Arthur. *Eyewitness Ancient China* (Eyewitness Books). DK Publishing, 2005.

Deady, Kathleen W., and Muriel L. Dubois. *Ancient China: Beyond the Great Wall* (FactFinders). Capstone Press, 2012.

Kopp, Megan. *Understanding Chinese Myths* (Myths Understood). Crabtree Publishing Company, 2012.

Matthews, Rupert, and Todd Van Pelt. *Ancient Chinese Civilization* (Ancient Civilizations and their Myths and Legends). Rosen Central, 2010.

National Geographic Essential Visual History of World Mythology. National Geographic Society, 2008.

Philip, Neil. *Eyewitness Mythology* (DK Eyewitness Books). DK Publishing, 2011.

Roberts, Jeremy. *Chinese Mythology A to Z* (Mythology A to Z). Chelsea House Publishers, 2010.

Shaughnessy, Edward L. *Exploring the Life, Myth, and Art of Ancient China* (Civilizations of the World). Rosen Publishing Group, 2010.

Sonneborn, Liz. *Ancient China* (The Ancient World). Scholastic, 2012.

Storrie, Paul D.. *Yu the Great: Conquering the Flood* (Graphic Myths and Legends). Graphic Universe, 2007.

Yang, Lihui and Deming An. *Handbook of Chinese Mythology* (Handbooks of World Mythology). Oxford University Press, 2008.

Yasuda, Anita. *The Jade Emperor: A Chinese Zodiac Myth* (Short Tales: Chinese Myths). Magic Wagon, 2014.

Yasuda, Anita. *The Monkey King: A Chinese Monkey Spirit Myth* (Short Tales: Chinese Myths). Magic Wagon, 2014.

Yasuda, Anita. *Pangu Separates the Sky from the Earth: A Chinese Creation Myth* (Short Tales: Chinese Myths). Magic Wagon, 2014.

Websites

http://www.godchecker.com/pantheon/chinese-mythology.php
A directory of Chinese deities from God Checker, written in a light-hearted style but with accurate information.

http://www.pantheon.org/areas/mythology/asia/chinese/
Encyclopedia Mythica page with links to many pages about Chinese myths. Click on the link to "available articles."

http://www.mythome.org/Asia.html
A page with links to different myths of Asia, including China, and an article on the Chinese pantheon.

http://www.crystalinks.com/china.html
This Crystal Links page has links to pages about all aspects of ancient China, including its gods, goddesses, and myths.

http://www.china.org.cn/english/daodejing-forum/208124.html
A page sponsored by the Chinese government that discusses ancient Chinese deities and immortals.

INDEX

PRONUNCIATION KEY	
Sound	**As in**
a	hat, map
ah	father, far
ai	care, air
aw	order
aw	all
ay	age, face
ch	child, much
ee	equal, see
ee	machine, city
eh	let, best
ih	it, pin, hymn
k	coat, look
o	hot, rock
oh	open, go
oh	grow, tableau
oo	rule, move, food
ow	house, out
oy	oil, voice
s	say, nice
sh	she, abolition
u	full, put
u	wood
uh	cup, butter
uh	flood
uh	about, ameba
uh	taken, purple
uh	pencil
uh	lemon
uh	circus
uh	labyrinth
uh	curtain
uh	Egyptian
uh	section
uh	fabulous
ur	term, learn, sir, work
y	icon, ice, five
yoo	music
zh	pleasure